Naseer Ahmad Habibi, Kudaibergenova Nur, Ulukbek Turdubekov

Electronic Waste mountain

GRIN Verlag

Bibliografische Information der Deutschen Nationalbibliothek:

Die Deutsche Bibliothek verzeichnet diese Publikation in der Deutschen National-bibliografie; detaillierte bibliografische Daten sind im Internet über http://dnb.d-nb.de/ abrufbar.

Dieses Werk sowie alle darin enthaltenen einzelnen Beiträge und Abbildungen sind urheberrechtlich geschützt. Jede Verwertung, die nicht ausdrücklich vom Urheberrechtsschutz zugelassen ist, bedarf der vorherigen Zustimmung des Verla-ges. Das gilt insbesondere für Vervielfältigungen, Bearbeitungen, Übersetzungen, Mikroverfilmungen, Auswertungen durch Datenbanken und für die Einspeicherung und Verarbeitung in elektronische Systeme. Alle Rechte, auch die des auszugsweisen Nachdrucks, der fotomechanischen Wiedergabe (einschließlich Mikrokopie) sowie der Auswertung durch Datenbanken oder ähnliche Einrichtungen, vorbehalten.

Impressum:

Copyright © 2013 GRIN Verlag GmbH
Druck und Bindung: Books on Demand GmbH, Norderstedt Germany
ISBN: 978-3-656-39881-3

Dieses Buch bei GRIN:

http://www.grin.com/de/e-book/211593/electronic-waste-mountain

American University of
Central Asia

Mathematics and Natural
Sciences Department

Clean Development Practice and
Policy Course

Team project report E-waste

Instructor: J. Martin

Team members: Kudaibergenova Nur-Peri,

Ulukbek Turdubekov, Naseer Ahmad

Brief summary: Following a brief description of the Electronic waste (E-waste) this project team report highlights the challenges and impacts of E-waste and discusses how sustainable management could protect the environment and human habitat.

Electronic Waste Mountain

Electronic waste (E-waste) is a complex mixture of hazardous and non-hazardous waste, which includes of items of economic value. Also the term electronic waste is known as 'redundant' or 'discarded' electronic devices, which are proved to be hazardous for the environment. These electronic devices are made of various components of metals, plastics and other substances including precious metals like gold, silver and copper as well as hazardous elements like mercury.

Over the past two decades, the global market of electrical and electronic equipment (EEE) has grown rapidly. This is largely due to what has been described as increasing market penetration of electronic products in developing countries, development of a replacement market in developed countries, and a generally high product obsolescence rate (Karin Lundgren, ILO, 2012, p.11). E-waste is now a big issue in both developed and developing countries. While the developed countries are trying to get rid of their E-wastes by exporting them to developing countries, this can equally cause damage to soil, water, air and nature as a whole. With the short lifespan of electronic products, businesses as well as waste management officials are facing a new challenge and E-waste or *waste electrical and electronic equipment* (WEEE) is receiving considerable amount of attention from stakeholders, mostly policy makers. Predictably the number of electrical devices will continue to increase at the global scale. Worldwide around 20 to 50 tons of E-waste is being generated annually (M. Khurrum S. Bhutta, Adnan Omar, 2011, p. 1).

Most people worldwide are unaware of the potential negative impacts of the rapidly increasing use of computers, monitors, and televisions. Meanwhile, "…certain components of electronic products contain toxic substances, which can generate a threat to the environment as well as to human health. For instance, television and computer monitors normally contain hazardous materials such as lead, mercury, and cadmium, while nickel, beryllium, and zinc can often be found in circuit boards." (M. KhurrumS. Bhutta, Adnan Omar, 2011, p. 1). All these hazardous and toxic substances are released into the environment due to the improper and unsatisfactory methods of recycling. As a result, people face serious health problems including birth defects, neurological disorders and reduced resistance to infections and cancer. Simultaneously, there are environmental losses, which are: contamination of water supplies, poisoning of the soil and destruction of habitat (William Cunningham, 2002, p.310). Due to the presence of these substances, recycling and disposal of E-waste becomes an important issue.

In light of the above issues, this paper explores answers to: what are the threats and negative impacts of E-waste toxic and hazardous substances to both human and environment; what should governments and businesses do to reduce the threat to human health and the environment from the increasing electronic wastes? Then, it clarifies what should be done by each individual in order to reduce the amount of E- waste? Afterward, it enlightens how E-waste can affect the environment and how does its primitive recycling in developing countries affect the health of men, women and children who do this without protection? Next, it explains what sustainable methods we could/should use in order to recycle or reuse E-wastes. Subsequently, it elucidates what should be done by companies which produce electronic items in order to reduce the amount of E- wastes? Finally, it discusses the methods of legal and illegal transfer of E-waste, and laws and regulations enforced by international environment community.

Nearly 80 % of the E-waste in developed countries which is supposed to be recycled ends up being shipped (often illegally) to developing countries such as China, India, Ghana and Nigeria for recycling. In these countries all components of E-waste are recycled manually, by people living in poverty - informal sector (Karin Lundgren, ILO, 2012, p.9). One of the researches in Taizhou, East China, where E-waste primitive recycling method (manual separation of substances, without any machinery) took place, showed high concentration of hazardous substances (mainly persistent organic pollutants (POPs), dioxins, furans) in air, soil, dust, sediment, freshwater, fish, and cow milk samples was two times higher than it was in other regions of East China, where e- waste was not recycled (Ashley, 2009, Web). The situation is similar with India, Brazil and Mexico where people are facing increasing health problems and environmental damage, because of leaving E-waste recycling to the "vagaries" of the informal sector (Karin Lundgren, ILO, 2012, p.19).

The research on increasing health problems in the last few years show that a lot of diseases and problems related to the skin, stomach, respiratory tract and other organs have been proved to be caused by E-waste. Workers in such environments suffer high incidences of birth defects, infant mortality, tuberculosis, blood diseases, anomalies in the immune system, malfunctioning of the kidneys and respiratory system, lung cancer, underdevelopment of the brain in children and damage to the nervous and blood systems, reproductive problems and even death (Karin Lundgren, ILO, 2012, p.20).

"Informal sector E-waste activities are also a crucial source of environment and food chain contamination, as contaminants may accumulate in agricultural lands and be available for uptake by grazing livestock...most chemicals of concern have a slow metabolic rate in animals, and may bioaccumulation in tissues and be excreted in edible products such as eggs and milk." (Karin Lundgren, ILO, 2012, p.20). All these contaminants, hazardous and toxic substances enter biological systems via food, water, air and soil (Deepti Mittal VSRD – IJCSIT, 2012, p.271). Later on, such toxic and hazardous enter the body of those workers of informal sector via inhalation, ingestion and skin absorption (Ashley, 2009, Web).

Children working as "scavengers" or "waste-pickers are particularly vulnerable to poisoning and threats posed by informal E-waste activities. The risks include more fatal and non-fatal accidents, permanent disabilities and/or ill health, and psychological, behavioral or emotional damage – can often be more devastating and lasting." (Karin Lundgren, ILO, 2012, p.21). Children at E-waste recycling sites are reported to be suffering from medical problems, such as: breathing ailments, skin infections and stomach diseases. Infants, due to their hand-to-mouth behavior, are one of the most vulnerable groups in areas where soils and dusts are contaminated with lead. In Guiyu, China, nearly 80 percent of children suffer from respiratory diseases. According to the *China Labour Bulletin*, "...E-waste recycling activities have contributed to elevated blood lead levels in children and high incidence of skin damage, headaches, vertigo, nausea, chronic gastritis, and gastric and duodenal ulcers." (Karin Lundgren, ILO, 2012, p.22)

The other issue of human risk is that those primitive methods of recycling (incineration/burning in open air, land filling/burial) disseminate geotaxis agents that threaten the health of current and future generations living in the local environment. Genotoxins are agents that damage the genetic material in cells, "...they are toxins that have been found to be mutagenic or carcinogenic, meaning they are capable of causing genetic mutations or the development of cancer" (Ashley, 2009, Web). These genotoxins include: metals, such as: chromium, beryllium, and cadmium; chlorinated dioxins and furans formed from the burning of plastics; and, flame retardants. The impact of these genotoxins on human cell's DNA or chromosomes can lead to a number of pathologies including genetic disorders, infertility, spontaneous abortions, elevated cancer risk and premature aging (Ashley, 2009, Web).

Another huge human risk is that these hazardous and toxic substances can travel long distances through air and water and to accumulate in our bodies and the environment (Deepti Mittal, VSRD – IJCSIT, 2012, p.273). Recent studies continue to discover the presence of POPs and other contaminants in environments where they have never been produced or even used before, indicating their ability to be transported over long-ranges. (Ashley, 2009, Web)

Because the variety of E-waste is increasing exponentially, many researches are still going on the question of; whether the effect/impact from interaction of chemicals, known as "the cocktail effect", can lead to more serious consequences rather than the effect/impact from the chemical individually? The answer is still ambiguous. The examples of "cocktail" are: multiple pesticides, diesel fumes, and other fumes and mixed solvents; chemicals are mixed with water. Exposed to sunlight in the air or dispersed within the complex chemistry of the soil. However, many scholars agreed that people impacted by "cocktail" are more likely to be or predisposed for disrupt hormonal systems, adversely affect on reproductive functions and causation of certain types of cancer. (Karin Lundgren, ILO, 2012, p.24)

Having read these devastating results presented above, it seems that, each person can understand that all of us are impacted by E – waste hazardous substances. The results of E-waste chemical's impact – all those illnesses (birth defects, neurological disorders, reduce resistance to infection, different types of cancer, problems related to the skin, stomach, respiratory tract, infant mortality, tuberculosis, blood diseases, anomalies in the immune system, malfunctioning of the kidneys, underdevelopment of child brain, damage to the nervous and blood systems, reproductive problems and even death), as well as the contamination of air, water, soil, food chain, flora and fauna – are caused by chemicals due to improper recycling methods. Taking into account that the amount of E-waste will be rapidly growing, we have to realize, that if effective methods of regulating E-waste are not undertaken by policymakers and each of us, there will be disastrous consequences, as for the present and future generations.

Despite the significant increase in the amount of the electronic waste, still some developing countries do not take it as a serious problem. Yearly our global E-waste generation is growing by about "40 million" tons. Governments should be very keen in reducing the amount of electronic waste in their countries. Nations can prevent or reduce the amount of electronic waste by taking the problem itself so serious. There are many ways that countries can do in order to reduce the threat to human health and the environment from the growing amount of E- waste. First, governments especially in developing countries should support and cooperate with UNEPs program regarding solid waste management. The UNEP project (ISWM) integrated solid waste management, "aims to promote identification and implementation environmentally sound technologies (ESTs) including collection, segregation, transportation, treatment, disposal, recovery and recycle" (*E- Waste Management Manual*, p.12, Pdf). The (ISWM) is based on the 3R (reduce, reuse and recycle) in urban areas of Asia pacific and Africa.

Therefore, the governments in mentioned regions should use as much as possible from the advice of the UNEP's team to have a sound and sustainable environment. Second, developed countries usually export their E-waste to the developing countries like; China, India, and some African countries. Here, the developing countries are suffering from the Wastes of developed nations. Subsequently, governments in developing countries can reduce or even ban the import of the electronic waste from developed countries by levying high taxes and tariffs. However, some states like China are keen to import the E- waste from other places in order to recycle it for making new items. Hence, by doing so China is facing a very dangerous environmental failure. Third, laws and regulations can be very effective tools of reducing the amount of E-waste. The companies that are functioning in a country without any doubt follows the rules, norms and laws of the government. So, governments should persuade the companies to increase the life cycle of their products, in order to reduce the amount of E- waste. This notion perhaps is the most effective way of reducing the quantity of electronic waste in the world if every nation agrees to do so.

It is commonly believed that if in a community each individual starts being green and sustainable, there is no doubt that the whole society will become green in a very short period of time, as Plato says, "If each person in a state commence to be a just person, there is now doubt that the whole state becomes a just state". However, the problem is that not everybody in a community has the same attitude, habits and feelings toward environment and being green. Those individuals who have the feelings of making some changes regarding environment or other issues have to pass the following stage to become effective. And individual can start being green from himself first, then community and finally society itself. Without implementing the principles of being green one on himself/herself, that won't work. Thus, the purpose of the whole paragraph is that an individual can affect the state starting from himself, whether in terms of waste or other issues.

Recycling is the most efficient way of conservation of resources and pollution reduction. However, in some least developed and developing countries that might turn out to be almost the opposite of not having environmentally sound technology (ESTs). Usually developing countries namely China, India Kenya and Brazil have very inefficient technology to recycle E- wastes. In

China and India E- waste is recycled in very harsh and harmful conditions, which have adverse effect not only on the lives of the workers, but also on the lives of their children. Basically or scientifically, there are three stages of recycling exist, which are: collection, dismantling or sorting and end processing, that include refining and disposal (*Recycling from E- waste to Resources*, p.38, pdf). The efficiency of the entire recycling chain depends on the efficiency of each step and on how well the interfaces between these interdependent steps are managed (*Recycling from E- waste to Resources,* p.38, pdf). First, collection stage is very crucial for the whole process because in this stage the whole collection should be enough to cover the cost of recycling. Many collection programs are the same, but their efficiency differs from place to place and also depends on the type of E- waste. Improvement of collection rates depends more on social and communal factors than on collection methods as such, but should be considered when discussing innovative recycling technology systems. When fewer devices are collected, the feed material to dismantling, preprocessing and end-processing facilities is lacking and a recycling chain cannot be established. The collected equipment is sorted and then enters a pre-treatment step (*Recycling from E- waste to Resources,* p.39, pdf). Second, the purpose of dismantling or pre-processing is to liberate the materials and direct them to adequate subsequent final treatment processes. Hazardous substances have to be removed and stored or treated safely while valuable components/materials need to be taken out for reuse or to be directed to efficient recovery processes. This includes removal of batteries, capacitors etc. prior to further (mechanical) pre-treatment. The batteries from the devices can be sent to dedicated facilities for the recovery of cobalt, nickel and copper. Third, in this stage each element that was sorted at the second stage transfers to its determined place and consists of three sub stages. First, "ferrous are directed to steel plants for recovery of iron" (*Recycling from E- waste to Resources,* p.40, pdf). Second, "aluminum fractions are going to aluminum smelter" (40). Third, "copper/lead fractions, circuits boards and other precious metal containing fractions are going to e.g. integrated metal smelter" (40). By doing so, the result would be the recovery of precious metal, copper and other non ferrous metals, while the hazardous substance are already isolated. Thus, the least developed or periphery and developing or semi periphery countries can use those three, mentioned recycling steps, to become more economically and environmentally sustainable. By doing so the recycling companies must insure and provide the updated safety for life of their recycler in order to avoid the adverse effect of waste.

In light of the above, the question rises; what are the objectives and goals of E- waste recycling and basic consideration for innovation. The following four basic objectives of recycling (*Recycling from E- waste to Resources,* p.42, pdf) if met can lead to sustainable recycling:

a. Taking care of hazardous/toxic substances contained in E-waste in an environmentally sound manner while preventing secondary and tertiary emissions.

b. Recovering valuable materials as effectively as possible.

c. Creating economically and environmentally sustainable businesses (optimize eco-efficiency).

d. Considering the social implications and the local context of operations (e.g. employment opportunities, available skills and education etc.).

Consequently, addressing these objectives a whole while respecting the nature, the recycling process would be successful and sustainable. Developing countries like; China and India do not take in to consideration at least two of the mentioned objectives. They do recover valuable materials as effectively as possible, but not in an environmentally sound manner. China does care about the growth of its economy; however, do not take the environment issues so serious. Annually China produces 6, 538,367,000 thousand of metric tons of carbon dioxide emissions, which is world's biggest polluter of the air. It produces 22.3% of the world Carbon dioxide emissions,

Any company, industry and business can be successful; if its output and the process of producing the output are based on environmentally friendly manners in the countries which care about its people, nature and environment. Unfortunately, some companies in Pakistan and Bangladesh have very low standard companies that take many lives each year. There are many ways that a business or industry can influence the quantity of its waste. First, companies which produce electronic items ought to invest on more sustainable technologies to reduce the amount of raw materials, which they used to produce goods and services. For instance, the computers that were produced 40 years ago are much bigger than the computers that we use now. By improvement of new technologies now those companies can produce more, however, using fewer resources. Second, companies like; Apple, Nokia, Honda, etc, which are the world's well-known companies can increase the life of their product in order to decrease the amount of its used items.

International trade and transportation of hazardous waste is one of key trends concerning the problem of E-waste. During the last decades amount of E-waste generation is increasing rapidly especially in developed countries. It costs much more to process E-waste within a country so most of the firms choose to send it out of the territory. Governments and environmental organizations try to control the flow of E-waste but they don't succeed sometimes. There is great amount shipping of E-waste from rich countries to poor and it is not always legal. There is several ways of transporting E-waste, the first is to export it legally if it is not in big amount, second, to transport it illegally by hiding it from reports, and the third, some exporters send their waste to poor countries by naming them as 'products for reuse' or 'donations', so their transfer is not counted in the overall report of export and import as hazardous waste. As Custom officials and police report, main exporters of E-waste are the USA and Europe and Hong Kong, China, Singapore and Malaysia are the main recipients in Asia and Nigeria and Ghana in Africa (Out of Control: E-waste trade flows from the EU to developing countries, p.8) In this part, we discuss amount of export and import depending on the country and some issues of laws and regulations.

First, we will talk about main exporters of toxic waste. According to The United Nations University (UNU), each citizen of Western Europe generates in average 14 to 24 kg of E-waste per year. In total, UNU proposes that 27 members of the European Union (EU) produced some 8.3 to 9.1 million tons of E-waste in 2005. "Currently, it is estimated that 25% of the medium sized appliances and 40% of the larger appliances are collected and treated. The rest, the remaining 60% to 75%, represents what Greenpeace International calls "the hidden flow". It might be stored or disposed of otherwise within the EU, but given the reports from developing countries parts of this "hidden flow" is being exported for reuse, recycling or disposal in, for example, Asia and Africa. Moreover, also some of the collected material might be exported to developing countries" (Out of Control: E-waste trade flows from the EU to developing countries, p.19).

In 2008, the US generated 3.16 million tons of e-waste. Of this amount, only 430,000 tons or 13.6 % was recycled, according to the Environmental Protection Agency (EPA). The rest was trashed – in landfills or incinerators (*E-waste, Facts and Figures*, and p.3). The Basel Action Network (BAN) and the Silicon Valley Toxics Coalition and Toxics Link revealed that because of high cost to dispose of E-waste responsibly at home, 50 to 80 percent of E-waste collected for recycling go to developing countries such as China, India and Pakistan.

And now we have a word about importers of E-waste. China is the first country in the world by hazardous waste import where ships with E-waste flood in daily mainly from the US, the EU, Japan and South Korea. In Guandong province there is a town Guiyu which is considered the biggest electronics dumping ground. As the town's website reported, 90% of Guiyu's industry comes from electronics recycling.

Nigeria is the dominant African importing country, followed by Ghana. "An analysis of 176 containers of two categories of used electrical and electronic equipment imported into Nigeria, conducted from March to July 2010, revealed that more than 75% of all containers came from Europe, approximately 15% from Asia, 5% from African ports (mainly Morocco) and 5% from North America. A similar distribution could be observed in Ghana, roughly 500 containers of electronics come per month, 85% of them originated in Europe, 4% in Asia, 8% in North America, and 3% from other destinations." (UNEP home page)

"Reflecting India's economic growth, roughly 333,000 metric tons was processed domestically in 2007, according to a study by an Indian industrial group, while 50,000 metric tons of E-waste still enters the country illegally each year. Bangalore operates a number of responsible recycling facilities where electronics are dismantled and sorted by hand." Joining a growing league of E-waste recipients, Indonesia has ideal geographical conditions to smuggling E-waste from West. It is hardly possible to monitor the flow of E-waste because of archipelago of much island.

Global environmental society being anxious about negative effect to environment of the enormous quantity of E-waste flowing and recycling by poor countries elaborated several laws, conventions and agreements. The most important multilateral agreement concerning E-waste is Basel convention. It was adopted on 22 March 1989 by the Conference of Plenipotentiaries which was convened at Basel from 20 to 22 March 1989. The majority of countries agreed and signed the convention except the USA. Later most of countries elaborated their programs and policies, amendments were also included in convention. One of them is the Ban Amendment to the Basel Convention that prohibits the export of hazardous waste from Organization for Economic Cooperation and Development (OECD) to non-OECD countries. It was adopted in 1995, but has yet to enter into force. Parties reaffirmed their support for the amendment at their 10th meeting in October 2011 by adopting a decision that is widely expected to speed the Ban Amendment's ratification and entry into force.

Main prohibitions and obligations of conventions are: restriction on the export (or import) of hazardous waste from (or to) non-party countries until it enters international agreement; ensure that generation of E-waste is at the minimum level; a requirement to prohibit persons within their jurisdictions from transporting hazardous wastes unless they are authorized to do so; obligations to require that hazardous waste exports are managed in an environmentally sound manner in the state of import. But restrictions on quantity exported and imported described in these agreements are inconsistent with General Agreement on Tariffs and trade

10

(GATT) which bars the institution or maintenance of quantitative restrictions on exports to, and imports from, any World Trade Organization (WTO) Member's territory. And WTO being institution of higher rank can strike down the ban or licensing system (Issues in International Trade Law: Restricting Exports of Electronic Waste, p.9). Since the 1980s, the United States has been a party to international agreements governing the trans-boundary movements of hazardous wastes. These agreements, one among the member countries of the OECD and two bilateral agreements with Canada and Mexico, condition hazardous waste exports on the notification of both exporting and destination countries and the destination country's consent (Issues in International Trade Law: Restricting Exports of Electronic Waste, p.1).

Kyrgyzstan became party of Basel Convention in 1996, creating the laws on limiting the quantity of E-waste produced and imported. National definition of hazardous waste is given in the Law of the Kyrgyz Republic from November 13, 2001 № 89 "On Waste from Production and Consumption". This law also regulates trans-boundary movements of hazardous waste. According to the law the control of E-waste is provided by the state bodies of executive power in charge of customs, ecological and sanitary-epidemiological control, one of the most important of them is the State Agency on Environment Protection and Forestry. To regulate the E-waste generation in Kyrgyzstan several policies are implemented. One of them is in the economic sphere through the following instruments:

- Fee (fees, taxes) for emissions;

- Payment for environmental violations;

- Civil liability. (Basel Convention Country Fact Sheet, Kyrgyzstan, p.2-4)

Table1.[1]

Data on the Generation and Trans-boundary Movements of Hazardous Wastes and other wastes in 2009		Quantities (in metric tons)
Generation	Amount of hazardous wastes generated under Art. 1(1)a (Annex I: Y1-Y45) of BC	
	Amount of hazardous wastes generated under Art. 1(1)b of BC	
	Total amount of hazardous wastes generated	
	Amount of other wastes generated (Annex II: Y46-Y47)	438,437
Export	Amount of hazardous wastes exported	1366
	Amount of other wastes exported	
Import	Amount of hazardous wastes imported	
	Amount of other wastes imported	

      The hazardous waste transfer issue reveals some key trends where TNCs are important actors in global environmental politics. First, the multinational companies are the first in exporting toxic waste, they make shift to hazardous waste exports for recycling and to transfer hazardous production processes. They contribute much to the problem of hazard relocation. Second, business lobby groups took a key role alongside NGOs in the negotiation of environment agreements regarding the waste trade. (Toxic Exports: The transfer of hazardous waste from rich to poor countries, p.18)

      To pass over on quantity restriction countries create different ways of transporting toxic waste for not being included in statistics. There is additional type of E-waste trade. It is trade of second-hand electronics, mostly bought by poor countries. However, the trade in second-hand electronics generates both positive and negative effects. On the one hand, it may increase poor people's access to IT and increase the lifespan of electronic items, which is good from an environmental point of view. On the other hand, the final disposal and treatment of the products

---

[1] Basel Convention Country Fact Sheet. Kyrgyzstan, p.10

will take place in countries where proper disposal and treatment systems are lacking. So after time passed it again generates E-waste in poor countries although it was not reported as hazardous waste transfer. (Out of Control: E-waste trade flows from the EU to developing countries, p.8)

As indicated, trade of E-waste through appropriate methods is profitable for both developed and developing countries as opposed to a unilateral damping approach. First, developed countries avoid high cost of domestic procession of E-waste while developing countries generate revenue and sometimes contribute to economic growth of their country. In some cities E-waste recycling composes the major part of industry. Because of these reasons in some countries laws are not efficient, because they transfer waste illegally out of statistics using different strategies. While each country acts for their own purpose and does not respect international agreements environment will continue to be destroyed by enormous E-waste mountains and its inefficient and inconsistent recycling. Second, developed countries usually export their E – waste to the developing countries like; China, India, and some African countries. Here, the developing countries are suffering from the Wastes of developed nations. Subsequently, governments in developing countries can reduce or even ban the import of the electronic waste from developed countries by levying high taxes and tariffs. However, some states like China are keen to import the E- waste from other places in order to recycle it for making new items. Hence, by doing so China is facing a very dangerous environmental failure. Third, laws and regulations can be very effective tools of reducing the amount of E- waste. The companies that are functioning in a country without any doubt follows the rules, norms and laws of the government. So, governments should persuade the companies to increase the life cycle of their products, in order to reduce the amount of E- waste. This notion perhaps is the most effective way of reducing the quantity of electronic waste in the world if every nation agrees to do so.

References:

1) William Cunningham, *Principles of environmental science.* University of Minnesota 2002, p. 303 – 309

2) Karin Lundgren (ILO consultant) – *The global impact of E-waste: addressing the challenge* / International Labour Office, Programme on Safety and Health at Work and the Environment (SafeWork), Sectoral Activities Department (SECTOR), Geneva 2012, p. 18 – 25

3) Deepti Mittal (Assistant Professor, Department of Information Technology) VSRD International Journal of Computer Science and Information technology. *E-waste : A Hidden Threat to Global Environment & Health* 2012, p. 272 – 274

4) Environmental Health Impacts of E-waste, http://health-E-waste.blogspot.com,2009, Web. 25 February, 2012

5) M. KhurrumS. Bhutta, Adnan Omar, and Xiaozhe Yang, *Research Article: ElectronicWaste: A Growing Concern in Today's Environment.* Hindawi Publishing Corporation Economics Research International Volume 2011,p. 2 – 5

6) Dittke, Susanne (Chemical Engineer/Environmental Consultant), "Presentation on the health and environmental impacts of E-waste". University Karlsruhe (Germany), South Africa, 2011

7) Mthias Schlup, *Recycling- From E- waste to Resources,* (July 2009, United Nation Environmental Program, United Nation University), pdf

8) UNEP, *E- Waste Management Manual,* Second Volume (2007United Nation Environmental Program), Pdf

9) Enger D. Eldon, Smith F. Bradley *Environmental Science,* seventh Edition (2000, McGraw-Hill Company Inc.), Book.

10) Bullock William, Scrogum Joy, 23 January 2013. Challenges. *Sustainable Electronic Initiative.* 15/02/2013, from http://www.sustainelectronics.illinois.edu

11) Emily C. Barbour *Issues in International Trade Law: Restricting Exports of Electronic Waste* (, Congressional Research Service [CRS] Reports, February 2012), pdf

12) Jennifer Clapp, *Toxic Exports: The Transfer of Hazardous waste from Rich to Poor Countries* (United States: Cornell University Press, 2001), book

13) Basel Convention Home Page

http://www.basel.int/Home/tabid/2202/mctl/ViewDetails/EventModID/8051/EventID/330/xmid/8052/Default.aspx

14) Sara Nordbrand, *Out of Control: E-waste trade flows from the EU to developing countries* (SwedWatch, April 2009)

15) Interactive map, E-waste transfer

http://www.pbs.org/frontlineworld/stories/ghana804/map/map.html

16) E-waste, facts and figures

http://www.epa.gov/epawaste/nonhaz/municipal/pubs/msw2008data.pdf

17) UNEP Home Page

http://www.unep.org/newscentre/default.aspx?DocumentID=2667&ArticleID=9022

18) Basel Convention Country Fact Sheet, Kyrgyzstan, doc